Contents

What is sunshine?

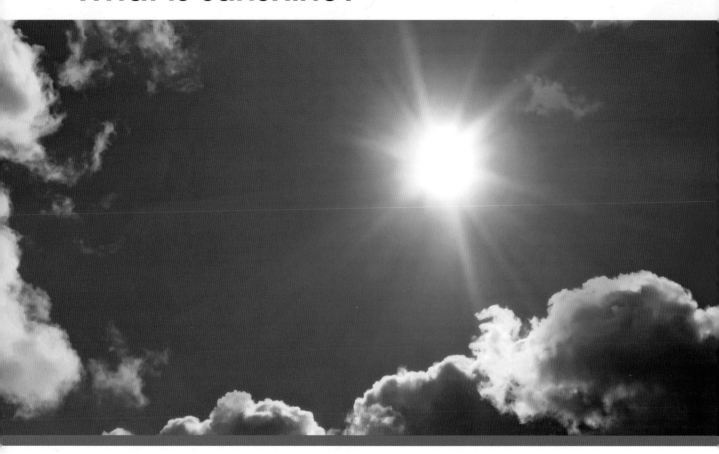

Sunshine is light from the Sun.

Weather Wise

Sunshine

Helen Cox Cannons

Raintree is an imprint of Capstone Global Library Limited, a company incorporated in England and Wales having its registered office at 7 Pilgrim Street, London, EC4V 6LB – Registered company number: 6695582

www.raintreepublishers.co.uk
myorders@raintreepublishers.co.uk

Edited by Siân Smith and John-Paul Wilkins
Designed by Philippa Jenkins
Picture research by Ruth Blair
Production by Victoria Fitzgerald
Originated by Capstone Global Library Ltd
Printed and bound in China

ISBN 978 1 4062 8480 5 (hardback)
18 17 16 15 14
10 9 8 7 6 5 4 3 2 1

ISBN 978 1 4062 8487 4 (paperback)
19 18 17 16 15
10 9 8 7 6 5 4 3 2 1

British Library Cataloguing in Publication Data
A full catalogue record for this book is available from the British Library.

Acknowledgements
We would like to thank the following for permission to reproduce photographs: Dreamstime: Gpointstudio, 19, Logoboom, 16; Getty Images: Maria Pavlova/E+, cover; iStockphoto: Alexander Chernyakov, 9, 23 (bottom), Kali Nine LLC, 14, konradlew, 10, skynesher, 21, Squaredpixels, 5, zeljkosantrac, 18; NASA: 12; Shutterstock: Africa Studio, 22 (sunscreen), bddigitalimages, 8, 23 (middle), hddigital, 6, 23 (top), Ivonne Wierink, 22 (hat), koosen, 22 (ball), Ljupco Smokovski, 22 (chair), Marques, 22 (duck), oneo, 4, Patrizia Tilly, 15, Stephen Lew, 17, Sunny Forest, 11, Tom Wang, 20, Vibrant Image Studio, 7

We would like to thank John Horel for his invaluable help in the preparation of this book.

Every effort has been made to contact copyright holders of material reproduced in this book. Any omissions will be rectified in subsequent printings if notice is given to the publisher.

Sunshine is very bright. Sunshine feels warm on your skin.

rising Sun

The Sun **rises** in the morning.
Then it becomes light outside.

During the day, the Sun moves across the sky.

The Sun **sets** in the evening.
Then it becomes dark outside.

You cannot see the Sun at night.

The Sun moves below the **skyline**.

The Sun heats the ocean.

The Sun heats the land.

The Sun

The Sun is a burning ball of gas.

Sunshine feels warm because it comes from the Sun.

Sunshine and the seasons

 Earth is closer to the Sun in summer. Summer days can be hot.

Earth is further away from the Sun in winter. Winter days can be cold.

Sunshine around the world

equator

Countries near the **equator** have very strong sunshine. These countries are often warm all year round.

16

Countries far from the equator
have very weak sunshine. These
countries are cold all year round.

Staying safe in the sun

 Sunshine can burn your skin. Wear sunscreen to stay safe in the sun.

Never look at the Sun. It can damage your eyes.

How does sunshine help us?

Sunshine helps plants grow.

Sunshine makes people feel happy!

Sunshine quiz

Which of these things will keep you safe in the sun?

beach chair

sun hat

sunscreen

beach ball

rubber duck

Answer: The sunscreen and the sun hat will keep you safe in the Sun.

Picture glossary

 equator imaginary circle around the middle of Earth

 rise to come up

 set to go down

 skyline the place where land and sky meet

Index

Notes for parents and teachers

Before reading

Assess background knowledge. Ask: What is sunshine? Where does sunshine come from? How does sunshine help us?

After reading

Recall and reflection: Ask children if their ideas about sunshine at the beginning were correct. What else do they wonder about?

Sentence knowledge: Ask children to look at page 16. How many sentences are on this page? How can they tell?

Word recognition: Ask children to point at the word *warm* on page 5. Can they also find it on page 13?